This Dialogue Journal Belongs to

Then the LORD answered
me and said,
"Write down the vision
And inscribe it clearly on
tablets, So that one who
reads it may run."
Habakkuk 2:2

THE AMERICAN STANDARD BIBLE

Heart to Heart

But First,

LET'S DIALOGUE

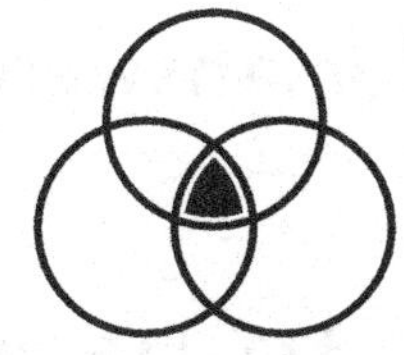

But First, Let's Dialogue Conversation Sequence

Prayer Definition

Scripture Reading

His Voice

Walking in the Dark

The God Head

Holy Spirit Read My Heart

Seeing Myself Through the Word

Speak to Me

Quiet Myself

Steps to Quiet Myself

My Quiet Experience

Speak to Me

Gratitude for Our Dialogue

Prayer Request

Thank You for Answered Prayer

Heart to Heart

Prayer is a Dialogue-
A Conversation between
you and God the Father,
Son, and Holy Spirit.

Speaking and listening opens
expansive communication
between you and God.

Read I Samuel 3:1-10

No one taught us what God's voice sounds like, so we do not recognize it when we hear it. We do not hear because our spiritual ear, heart, and mind is not tuned to hear His Voice.

Read: I Kings 19:11-13

WALKING IN THE DARK

The next time you pray
Quiet yourself
and let
God the Father,
God the Son,
and
Holy Spirit
do most of the talking.

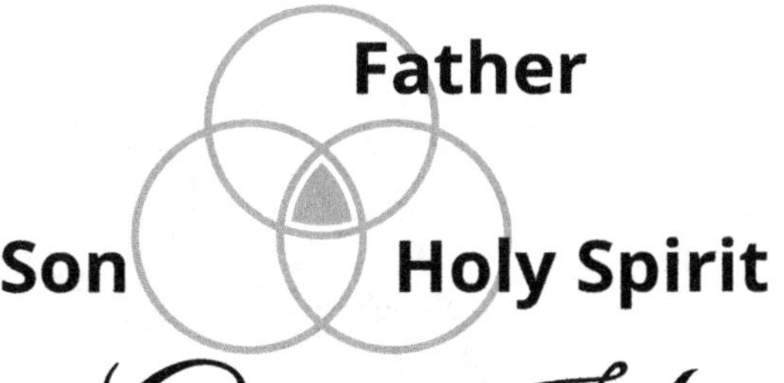

The God Head

Father

F-

S-

L-

Son(Jesus)

F-

S-

L-

Holy Spirit

F-

S-

L-

Time in the Word:

- GENESIS 1 & 2;
- PSALM 32:8-9;
- I TIMOTHY 3:16;
- COLOSSIANS 2:9;
- JOHN 10:30;15:26; 16:13-14;
- I JOHN 3:1-4; REVELATION 3:20; MATTHEW 13:16-17;
- II TIMOTHY 3:16-17

Read the scriptures below and choose one word from the terms provided to describe the (F) Function, (S) Status, and (L) Location of the God Head! Matthew 6:9-13, 29:19 Acts 4:12; John 3:16; Luke 22:69, John 14:16-18,
Use the terms provided: Helper, Savior, Provider, Heaven, Set Apart (Holy), Active, Seated, Earth,

- God provided everything in 6 days, rested the seventh day, and waiting on us to discover what He provided.
- Big brother took our punishment died and rose on the 3rd day.
- Holy Spirit is not an extra-He is Essential.

Let the Holy Spirit read your heart while you read the Bible.
Dialogue with scripture ask the Holy Spirit to open the word of God for you.
Let it become the living word that addresses, guide, and speak to you. Waiting for a response from Him.

Read Psalms 139:1-24

Seeing Myself In the Word!

Write one word on the lines below how the Word see you.

_Ask God for your Scripture Reading:_________________________

Hebrews 4:12; Isaiah 55:11; I Thessalonians 2:13

Write on the sticky notes below the line how you see yourself.

Seeing Myself in the Word / /

"Search me, O God, and know my heart; try me, and know my thoughts; and see if there be any wicked way in me, and lead me in the way everlasting." Psalm 139:23-24

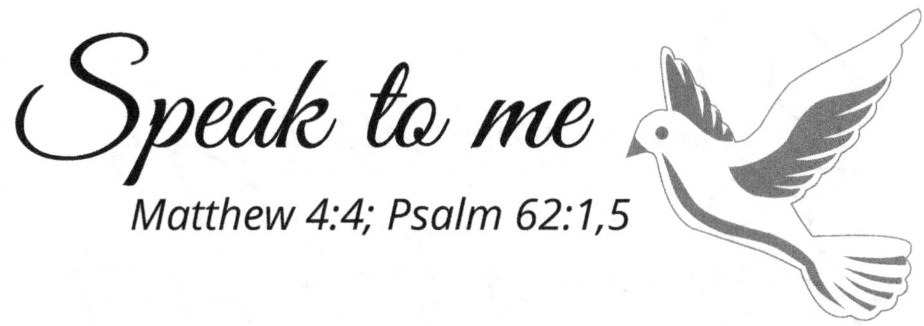

Quiet yourself in the presence of the Holy Spirit!

Quiet yourself in the Presence of the Holy Spirit, Block everything out, and listen carefully. Schedule time if you are not accustomed to this. Quiet your soul (head) and let your spirit (heart) do the talking and listening.

Read Luke 5:16

Speak to me

Quiet yourself in the presence of the Holy Spirit!

My Quiet Experience / /

God speaks to everybody

"When the student is ready the teacher will appear." *Acts 8:29-31*

Stepping Into the Light

Let the Holy Spirit read your heart while you read the Bible. Dialogue with scripture ask the Holy Spirit to open the word of God for you. Let it become the living word that addresses, guide, and speak to you. Waiting for a response from Him.

Read St. John 6:41-51

Seeing Myself In the Word!

Write one word on the lines below how the Word see you.

Write on the sticky notes below the line how you see yourself.

Seeing Myself in the Word / /

"Search me, O God, and know my heart; try me, and know my thoughts; and see if there be any wicked way in me, and lead me in the way everlasting." Psalm 139:23-24

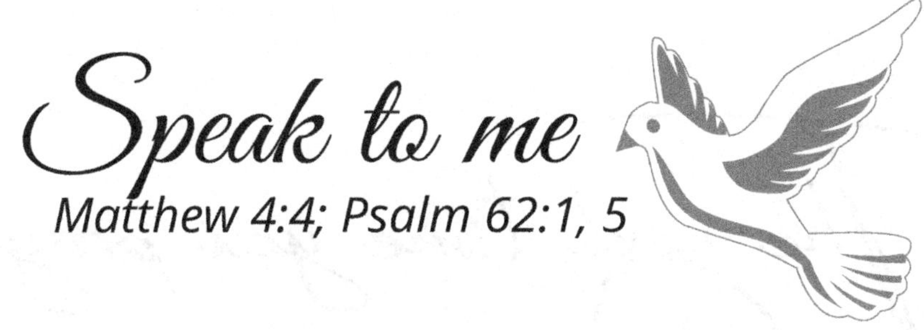

Quiet yourself in the presence of the Holy Spirit!

The next time you pray
Quiet yourself
and let
God the Father,
God the Son,
and
Holy Spirit
do most of the talking.

Quiet yourself in the Presence of the Holy Spirit, Block everything out, and listen carefully. Treat the distractions like the dog that barks next door, Acknowledge it and Let it go.

Read Matthew 11:15

Speak to me

Quiet yourself in the presence of the Holy Spirit!

My Quiet Experience / /

God speaks to everybody

"When the student is ready the teacher will appear." St. John 10:3-4

Gratitude for Our Dialogue

PRAYER REQUEST

Jeremiah 33:3

Asked and Answered

Thank You for Answered Prayer

"One thing have I desired of the Lord, that will I seek after; that I may dwell in the house of the Lord all the days of my life, to behold the beauty of the Lord, and to inquire in his temple."

Psalm 27:4

Stepping
Into the
Light

Let the Holy Spirit read your heart while you read the Bible.
Dialogue with scripture ask the Holy Spirit to open the word of God for you.
Let it become the living word that addresses, guide, and speak to you. Waiting for a response from Him.

Read I Kings 19:9-13

Seeing Myself In the Word!

Write one word on the lines below how the Word see you.

Write on the sticky notes below the line how you see yourself.

Seeing Myself in the Word / /

"Search me, O God, and know my heart; try me, and know my thoughts; and see if there be any wicked way in me, and lead me in the way everlasting." Psalm 139:23-24

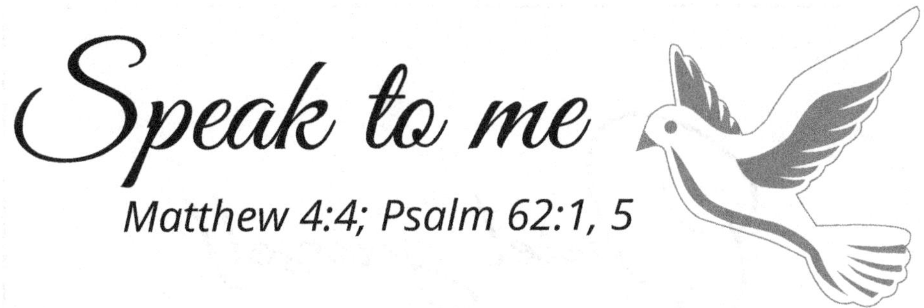

Quiet yourself in the presence of the Holy Spirit!

Quiet yourself
let
God the Father,
Son, and
Holy Spirit
do most of the talking.

Quiet yourself in the Presence of the Holy Spirit, Block everything out, and listen carefully. Schedule time if you are not accustomed to this. Quiet your soul (head) and let your spirit (heart) do the talking and listening.

Read Matthew 11:15

Speak to me

Quiet yourself in the presence of the Holy Spirit!

My Quiet Experience / /

God speaks to everybody

"When the student is ready the teacher will appear." Matthew 4:4

Gratitude for Our Dialogue

PRAYER REQUEST

Ephesians 3:14-15

Asked and Answered

Thank You for Answered Prayer

"One thing have I desired of the Lord, that will I seek after; that I may dwell in the house of the Lord all the days of my life, to behold the beauty of the Lord, and to inquire in his temple."
Psalm 27:4

Stepping
Into the
Light

Let the Holy Spirit read your heart while you read the Bible.
Dialogue with scripture ask the Holy Spirit to open the word of God for you.
Let it become the living word that addresses, guide, and speak to you. Waiting for a response from Him.

Read: II Corinthians 5:17-19

Seeing Myself In the Word!

Write one word on the lines below how the Word see you.

Write on the sticky notes below the line how you see yourself.

Seeing Myself in the Word / /

"Search me, O God, and know my heart; try me, and know my thoughts; and see if there be any wicked way in me, and lead me in the way everlasting." Psalm 139:23-24

Quiet yourself
and let
God the Father,
Son, and
Holy Spirit
do most of the talking.
Draw a picture or
impression that
He brings to mind.

Speak to me

Matthew 4:4; Psalm 62:1, 5

Quiet yourself in the presence of the Holy Spirit!

Quiet yourself in the Presence of God the Father, Son, and Holy Spirit.

Write the words of a song that He places on your heart and meditate on the words.

Read St. John 7:37-39

Speak to me

Quiet yourself in the presence of the Holy Spirit!

My Quiet Experience / /

God speaks to everybody

"When the student is ready the teacher will appear." *Acts 8:29-31*

Gratitude for Our Dialogue

PRAYER REQUEST

Psalms 31:10-12

Asked and Answered

Thank You for Answered Prayer

"One thing have I desired of the Lord, that will I seek after; that I may dwell in the house of the Lord all the days of my life, to behold the beauty of the Lord, and to inquire in his temple."
Psalm 27:4

Stepping Into the Light

Let the Holy Spirit read your heart while you read the Bible. Dialogue with scripture ask the Holy Spirit to open the word of God for you. Let it become the living word that addresses, guide, and speak to you. Waiting for a response from Him.

Read Jeremiah 33:3

Seeing Myself In the Word!

Write one word on the lines below how the Word see you.

Write on the sticky notes below the line how you see yourself.

Seeing Myself in the Word / /

"Search me, O God, and know my heart; try me, and know my thoughts; and see if there be any wicked way in me, and lead me in the way everlasting." Psalm 139:23-24

Speak to me

Matthew 4:4; Psalm 62:1, 5

Quiet yourself in the presence of the Holy Spirit!

Quiet yourself in
Prayer and let
God the Father,
Son, and
Holy Spirit
do most of the talking.
Spend time in nature.

Quiet yourself in the Presence of the Holy Spirit, Block everything out, and listen carefully. Schedule time if you are not accustomed to this. Quiet your soul (head) and let your spirit (heart) do the talking and listening

Read Hebrews 4:12

Speak to me

Quiet yourself in the presence of the Holy Spirit!

My Quiet Experience / /

God speaks to everybody

"When the student is ready the teacher will appear." *Acts 17:11*

Gratitude for Our Dialogue

PRAYER REQUEST

James 5:13; I Thessalonians 5:16-18

Asked and Answered

Thank You for Answered Prayer

"One thing have I desired of the Lord, that will I seek after; that I may dwell in the house of the Lord all the days of my life, to behold the beauty of the Lord, and to inquire in his temple."
Psalm 27:4

WALKING IN THE DARK

Let the Holy Spirit read your heart while you read the Bible.
Dialogue with scripture
ask the Holy Spirit to open the word of God for you.
Let it become the living word that addresses, guide, and speak to you.
Waiting for a response from Him.

Read St. John 10:27

Seeing Myself: In the Word!

Write one word on the lines below how the Word see you.

Write on the sticky notes below the line how you see yourself.

Seeing Myself in the Word / /

"Search me, O God, and know my heart; try me, and know my thoughts; and see if there be any wicked way in me, and lead me in the way everlasting." Psalm 139:23-24

Speak to me

Matthew 4:4; Psalm 62:1, 5

Quiet yourself in the presence of the Holy Spirit!

Quiet yourself in
Prayer and let
God the Father,
Son, and
Holy Spirit
do most of the talking.
Write down the scripture
that He brings to mind.

Quiet yourself in the Presence of the Holy Spirit, Block everything out, and listen carefully. Schedule time if you are not accustomed to this. Quiet your soul (head) and let your spirit (heart) do the talking and listening.

Read Romans 10:17

Speak to me

Quiet yourself in the presence of the Holy Spirit!

My Quiet Experience / /

God speaks to everybody

"When the student is ready the teacher will appear." *Acts 8:29-31*

Gratitude for Our Dialogue

PRAYER REQUEST

Luke 6:27-28

Asked *and* *Answered*

Thank You for Answered Prayer

"One thing have I desired of the Lord, that will I seek after; that I may dwell in the house of the Lord all the days of my life, to behold the beauty of the Lord, and to inquire in his temple."

Psalm 27:4

WALKING IN THE DARK

Let the Holy Spirit read your heart while you read the Bible.
Dialogue with scripture ask the Holy Spirit to open the word of God for you.
Let it become the living word that addresses, guide, and speak to you.
Waiting for a response from Him.

Read Psalms 139:1-24

Seeing Myself In the Word!

Write one word on the lines below how the Word see you.

Write on the sticky notes below the line how you see yourself.

Seeing Myself in the Word / /

"Search me, O God, and know my heart; try me, and know my thoughts; and see if there be any wicked way in me, and lead me in the way everlasting." Psalm 139:23-24

Speak to me

Matthew 4:4; Psalm 62:1,5

Quiet yourself in the presence of the Holy Spirit!

Quiet Yourself in Prayer and let God the Father, Son, and Holy Spirit do most of the talking.

What is He saying to You?

Read II Corinthians 10:5

Speak to me

Quiet yourself in the presence of the Holy Spirit!

My Quiet Experience / /

God speaks to everybody

"When the student is ready the teacher will appear." *Acts 8:29-31*

Gratitude for Our Dialogue

PRAYER REQUEST

Jeremiah 32: 17, 27

Asked and Answered

Thank You for Answered Prayer

"One thing have I desired of the Lord, that will I seek after; that I may dwell in the house of the Lord all the days of my life, to behold the beauty of the Lord, and to inquire in his temple."
Psalm 27:4

Stepping
Into the
Light

Let the Holy Spirit read your heart while you read the Bible.
Dialogue with scripture ask the Holy Spirit to open the word of God for you.
Let it become the living word that addresses, guide, and speak to you. Waiting for a response from Him.

Read Psalms 139:1-24

Seeing Myself: In the Word!

Write one word on the lines below how the Word see you.

Write on the sticky notes below the line how you see yourself.

Seeing Myself in the Word / /

"Search me, O God, and know my heart; try me, and know my thoughts; and see if there be any wicked way in me, and lead me in the way everlasting." Psalm 139:23-24

Speak to me

Matthew 4:4; Psalm 62:1,5

Quiet yourself in the presence of the Holy Spirit!

The next time you pray
Quiet yourself
and let
God the Father,
God the Son,
and
Holy Spirit
do most of the talking.

Quiet yourself in the Presence of the Holy Spirit, Block everything out, and listen carefully. Schedule time if you are not accustomed to this. Quiet your soul (head) and let your spirit (heart) do the talking and listening.

Read Psalm 46:10

Speak to me

Quiet yourself in the presence of the Holy Spirit!

My Quiet Experience / /

God speaks to everybody

"When the student is ready the teacher will appear." *Acts 8:29-31*

Gratitude for Our Dialogue

PRAYER REQUEST

Luke 2:14; Psalm 9:10

Asked and Answered

Thank You for Answered Prayer

"One thing have I desired of the Lord, that will I seek after; that I may dwell in the house of the Lord all the days of my life, to behold the beauty of the Lord, and to inquire in his temple."

Psalm 27:4

WALKING IN THE DARK

Let the Holy Spirit read your heart while you read the Bible.

Dialogue with scripture ask the Holy Spirit to open the word of God for you.

Let it become the living word that addresses, guide, and speak to you.

Waiting for a response from Him.

Read St. John 10:27

Seeing Myself In the Word!

Write one word on the lines below how the Word see you.

Write on the sticky notes below the line how you see yourself.

Seeing Myself in the Word / /

"Search me, O God, and know my heart; try me, and know my thoughts; and see if there be any wicked way in me, and lead me in the way everlasting." Psalm 139:23-24

Speak to me

Matthew 4:4; Psalm 62:1, 5

Quiet yourself in the presence of the Holy Spirit!

Quiet yourself in
Prayer and let
God the Father,
Son, and
Holy Spirit
do most of the talking.
Write down the scripture
that He brings to mind.

Quiet yourself in the Presence of the Holy Spirit, Block everything out, and listen carefully. Schedule time if you are not accustomed to this. Quiet your soul (head) and let your spirit (heart) do the talking and listening.

Read Romans 10:17

Speak to me

Quiet yourself in the presence of the Holy Spirit!

My Quiet Experience / /

God speaks to everybody

"When the student is ready the teacher will appear." *Acts 8:29-31*

Gratitude for Our Dialogue

PRAYER REQUEST

Luke 6:27-28

Asked and Answered

Thank You for Answered Prayer

"One thing have I desired of the Lord, that will I seek after; that I may dwell in the house of the Lord all the days of my life, to behold the beauty of the Lord, and to inquire in his temple."

Psalm 27:4

WALKING IN THE DARK

Let the Holy Spirit read your heart while you read the Bible.
Dialogue with scripture ask the Holy Spirit to open the word of God for you.
Let it become the living word that addresses, guide, and speak to you.
Waiting for a response from Him.

Read Psalms 139:1-24

Seeing Myself In the Word!

Write one word on the lines below how the Word see you.

Write on the sticky notes below the line how you see yourself.

Seeing Myself in the Word / /

"Search me, O God, and know my heart; try me, and know my thoughts; and see if there be any wicked way in me, and lead me in the way everlasting." Psalm 139:23-24

Speak to me

Matthew 4:4; Psalm 62:1,5

Quiet yourself in the presence of the Holy Spirit!

Quiet Yourself in Prayer and let God the Father, Son, and Holy Spirit do most of the talking.

What is He saying to You?

Read II Corinthians 10:5

Speak to me

Quiet yourself in the presence of the Holy Spirit!

Made in the USA
Middletown, DE
30 September 2024